How To Create Your Purpose Driven, Highly Profitable Personal Brand!

WIN ALL DAY

PERSONAL BRANDING

Coach JC

Johnathan Conneely

WWW.COACHJC.COM

Mention of specific companies, organizations, or authorities in this book does not imply endorsement by the author or publisher, nor does mention of specific companies, organizations, or authorities imply that they endorse this book, its author, or the publisher.

Internet addresses, telephone numbers, names and titles given in this book were accurate at the time it went to press.

JJC ENTERPRISES
8177 S Harvard Ave.
Suite 420
Tulsa OK 74137
www.CoachJC.com

All rights reserved. No part of this publication may be reproduced or transmitted in any form or by any means, electronic or mechanical, including photocopying, recording, or any other information storage and retrieval system, without the written permission of the publisher.

While all attempts have been made to verify information provided in this book and its ancillary materials, neither the author nor publisher assumes any responsibility for errors, inaccuracies or omissions. Any slights of people or organizations are unintentional.

The purpose of this book is to educate and entertain. The author or publisher does not guarantee that anyone following the ideas, tips, suggestions, techniques or strategies will become successful. The author and publisher shall assume no liability or responsibility to anyone with respect to any loss or damage caused, or alleged to be caused, directly or indirectly, by the information contained in this book.

Cover and Layout Design by aspiretodesign.com

ISBN: 9780578781655

Printed in the United Stated of America

This book is dedicated to my family, friends and all the people that choose compassion, love, positivity, hard work and the desire to WIN.

YOU WERE BORN A WINNER!

YOU CAN WIN!

YOU WILL WIN!

YOU MUST WIN!

WIN ALL DAY!

CONTENTS

Section One: WHO. Who Are You? Who Do You Serve?
Lesson 1: WINNING MINDSET 30
Lesson 2: WHO ARE YOU 35
Lesson 3: DON'T ACCEPT FAILURE 40
Lesson 4: NO MORE EXCUSES 42
Lesson 5: LET NEGATIVITY GO 43
Lesson 6: DETERMINE YOUR ATTITUDE 45
Lesson 7: WHO DO I SERVE 47
Lesson 8: WHAT'S YOUR STORY 50

Section Two: WHAT. Create Your Vision. Create Your Offer.
Lesson 9: WINNING STARTS WITH DESIRE 54
Lesson 10: CHANGE YOUR THINKING 56
Lesson 11: MY PASSION IS 58
Lesson 12: DON'T FEAR FAILURE 60
Lesson 13: KNOWLEDGE IS POWER 62
Lesson 14: THINK BIG 64
Lesson 15: THE BIG 3 66
Lesson 16: THROW THE LID OFF 68
Lesson 17: YOUR IRRESISTIBLE OFFER 70

Section Three: WHY. Discover Your Purpose. Create Your Movement.
Lesson 18: KNOW YOUR PURPOSE 74
Lesson 19: GET BACK IN THE GAME 76
Lesson 20: OBSTACLES CREATE OPPORTUNITY 78
Lesson 21: TAKE BACK THE POWER 80
Lesson 22: BUILD A MOVEMENT 82
Lesson 23: NEVER QUIT 84

Lesson 24: EXPECT RESULTS 86
Lesson 25: PRIORITIES 88

PLAYBOOK: Make It A Reality.
Lesson 26: WHAT'S YOUR GAMEPLAN 92
Lesson 27: TAKE ACTION 94
Lesson 28: ARE YOU ACCOUNTABLE 96
Lesson 29: SENSE OF URGENCY 98
Lesson 30: WHAT YOU SOW YOU SHALL REAP 100
Lesson 31: GOALS 102
Lesson 32: SPEAK IT 104
Lesson 33: MAKE THE DECISION 107
Lesson 34: JUST DO IT 110

YOU have a story to tell! YOU are the MVP! Everything you have been through has led you to this point in your life. The messes, the successes, the trials, the storms, the obstacles, the hardships, the victories, the triumphs, all of the highs and lows. It all had to happen and it was all preparation for this moment in time.

There is one thing you have that no one else has in the entire world. YOU! That's right! You are unique and you were born with a purpose! You are here on purpose! No one has your story and now is your time to take it and share it with the world and make your greatest impact. How?

YOU! By you becoming an AUTHORITY! An EXPERT! Helping people solve their problems, adding tremendous value to this world, and getting paid to do so. The internet is your playing field! College is being replaced by the internet and the Information/knowledge business is an over $100 billion dollar industry.

THE GREATEST business to start right now is your PERSONAL BRAND! Taking what you know, what you have been through, packaging it, finding the right people to buy it, and selling it. People are looking for someone like you, what you know, what you do, your skills/knowledge in order to help them WIN.

This book is for you if…

YOU WANT TO REINVENT YOURSELF, BE A SPEAKER, COACH, CONSULTANT, WRITE A BOOK, START A PODCAST, AND GET YOUR MESSAGE TO THE WORLD.

Maybe you have had success as a business owner or CEO and are now entering a new season of life. You desire to wake up with purpose and be able give back and serve. You had great success in your career, you reached the pinnacle but feel unfilled and want this next season of life to be purpose driven. You have an idea, goal, or dream but haven't been able to bring it to reality.

YOU ARE STUCK WORKING A JOB BUT UNFULFILLED AND UNSATISFIED.

You are stuck making a living but haven't been able to make a life. You want to build a life with the freedom to spend more time with your family, take vacations, and do life on your terms. You desire to do what you are passionate about and profit from it. You have a skill or a trait and you would love to teach other people how to do it and get paid while doing it. You desire to experience freedom and fulfillment in life.

YOUR BACK IS AGAINST THE WALL AND YOU ARE SICK AND TIRED OF STRUGGLING FINANCIALLY.

During this time of uncertainty, worry, fear and doubt your back is against the wall and you need an answer for a business, an answer for creating some financial freedom in life. You see people use their skills and knowledge as a business but just never knew how it could be possible. The answer is by building your personal brand and creating security for you and your family. You know there is more out there but because of fear and lack of resources, you haven't been able to tap into it.

YOU HAVE A STORY TO TELL AND FEEL CALLED WITH A MISSION AND PURPOSE.

You went through a traumatic situation, hit rock bottom, or an obstacle in life took your hope and, like me, took you to a dark place. And you would like to take that mess and make it your message. Take that trial and make it your testimony. Take that loss and flip it into a WIN. Take that most painful moment and make it your purpose! You have a message that you know God has put in your heart that you want to share with the world.

MAKE YOUR GREATEST IMPACT!
Success without fulfillment is the ultimate failure!

Many people are so busy making a living that they haven't been able to make a life. We spend most of our lives working a job and hating it. Many people go through life unfulfilled and unhappy, which leads to an emptiness, and over time leads to burn out, health issues, relationship struggles, financial burdens, and the constant battle of living life with regret; asking ourselves, "What if...?!" or "If only...?!"

You don't have to aimlessly go through each day with no drive, just surviving and just getting by. You don't have to continually wake up dreading another day, doing work that makes you feel uninspired with your only motivation in getting to the weekend.

You can experience abundance, happiness and fulfillment in life... and it comes from PURPOSE. **PURPOSE** brings **PASSION!** You can do what you love and make money doing it!

It's time to make your **GREATEST IMPACT**. It's time to do life on your terms. To create a NEW STORY for your life! A new way of living your life, a new reality. A life with more PASSION fueled by PURPOSE! A life where you are making your greatest impact on the world, loving what you are doing, fulfilled and happy, and **HIGHLY PROFITABLE!**

The world NEEDS what you have! You were born with a **PURPOSE**. You were created for a reason. You have a message and a MISSION! You will fulfill your destiny!

CREATE TIME AND FINANCIAL FREEDOM.

The world may seem uncertain at times with many unknowns. There are times of uncertainty with emotional highs and lows. These times are also defining moments for you! With every obstacle comes an opportunity.

This is a defining moment in your life... To take an obstacle

and flip it into an opportunity. And that opportunity is betting on YOU! It's you going ALL IN on YOU! There is no greater asset than YOU! YOU are the MVP! You have a skillset, knowledge, or an idea that you can sell for money. You have been through trials, storms, and hardships in life that you're able to show others how to overcome and get paid to do so. You have done things that are impressive and you can consult or coach others to do and trade your value and get paid to do so.

A MESSAGE FROM COACH JC

"When you live a life of purpose, passion and true fulfillment will follow. Your Personal Brand is built through your purpose and this will bring passion so you can WIN in life!"

Coach JC

Hey WINNER,

You are holding in your hand, not only a book, but most importantly, a blueprint. A blueprint for you to create your new reality and orchestrate your future. I am a walking miracle, a comeback kid, from rags to riches story but most importantly, I am a walking testimony. A testimony for you to become motivated, inspired, and encouraged that if I can do it, you can too! I have been blessed to do what I love to do and make a living doing it. That is helping people build a purpose-filled life, profit from their passions and ultimately WIN IN LIFE! But it all started in 2003 when I laid face down in my apartment, in the fight of my life. Fighting to be a father, in a custody battle that brought me to over $400k in debt, ended with me depressed, oppressed, down and out, and suicidal. I made a decision at that moment in time to create a new story for my life. I did some strategic things at the time to pull me out of the dark place I was in and create my new reality.

That is just a small part of my story but in creating that new story for my life I also discovered that everything I went through HAD TO HAPPEN and my most painful moments in life became my GREATEST PURPOSE!

This book you are holding is 17 years in the making and is based off of real life trial and error. Not theory, not something I think is a good idea, but the blueprint that I used in my own life to create a personal brand. The same game plan that has helped others take their story, knowledge, and skillsets and create their PURPOSE driven life and HIGHLY PROFITABLE personal brand. And YOU ARE NEXT!

It's the systems from marketing, sales, fulfillment, etc. that most people believe make up a successful business but none of these things work without a BRAND. Your personal brand is what will drive your purpose and fuel your passion so that you can reach the people you are called to reach, make your greatest impact, and make a living doing it.

This book is compiled of a few of the most important things I did to create a purpose driven life and build my personal brand, "Coach JC", The "WIN ALL DAY" movement, and four other brands are built around my personal brand. My personal brand has been the thing that has allowed me to experience a life of abundance and true fulfillment. I believe that this will serve you the same way it did me and thousands of other people before you.

I am believing THE BEST for you, and as you implement this game plan I pray that you will experience a life of over-the-top passion, joy, strength, peace, love, positivity, intensity, motivation, inspiration, encouragement, giving, impact, and happiness... a PURPOSE-DRIVEN, PASSION-FILLED, HIGHLY PROFITABLE LIFE!

WIN ALL DAY!

Coach JC

Founder & CEO

For more resources, videos and strategies to be your best and WIN more in life, visit CoachJC.com

WIN ALL DAY

You were born a WINNER! You can WIN! You will WIN!

The only thing keeping you from getting what you really want in life is the story you keep telling yourself of why you don't have it.

To create a new story, I had to create a new belief. You don't get what you want in life, you get who you believe you are!

One of the greatest beliefs in life is the belief in YOU! Who You Were Born To Be! Who You Are! And Who You Can Become! Change your belief… Change your life!

Start to assign new meaning to your life, a new story so that you can create a new belief.

When we create a word, we give it meaning and create a new way of thinking. The words we use create our reality!

"WIN ALL DAY!"

WIN = You were born a WINNER. You can WIN. You will WIN. You must WIN. "I am here on PURPOSE!" "I have a PURPOSE!"

ALL DAY = ALL THINGS! ALL things are possible! ALL things work together for good!

WIN ALL DAY is a BELIEF! It's a MINDSET that today is your day! "NOTHING will get in the way of me being THE BEST version of myself!"

It is a DECISION. To be on a constant pursuit to walk out your calling, purpose, mission, and ultimately fulfill your destiny. "I CREATE MY REALITY!"

A decision each day that "I CAN DO ALL THINGS!" To be your best, physically, mentally, emotionally, spiritually, relationally, and financially! "I AM strong!" "I AM passionate!"

A decision that no matter the situation, the circumstance, the trial and storms of life that ALL things work together for good!

"I AM FEARLESS!" "I choose FAITH!" I choose a relentless, positive, passionate, confident, intense, deliberate, joyful, encouraging, inspiring, motivating, purpose-driven attitude. One of certainty, expectancy, and EXCELLENCE!

Today you take on a new belief! You create a new story for your life…

And that belief is, "WIN ALL DAY!"

"I WAS BORN A WINNER!" "I WILL WIN AND WIN ALL DAY"

Here is your WIN ALL DAY WINNING Confession:

WIN ALL DAY

TODAY IS MY DAY
NOTHING WILL GET IN MY WAY
OF ME BEING THE BEST VERSION OF ME
I AM HERE ON PURPOSE
I HAVE A PURPOSE
I AM STRONG
I AM PASSIONATE
I AM FEARLESS
I CHOOSE FAITH
I AM A WINNER
I WILL WIN AND WIN ALL DAY

SEE IT. SAY IT. SEE IT.

1. **SEE IT** – See this WINNING confession at least three times per day.
2. **SAY IT** – Say it at least three times per day with conviction and authority.
3. **SEE IT** – Visualize yourself already there, your new belief, story, you WINNING!

WINNING IS BUILT ON WINNING

WINNING IS BUILT ON WINNING! Many people hope and wish to WIN but never WIN. Many people watch others WIN and desire to WIN but never WIN.

WINNING is built by producing small wins over and over again. I call it **STACKING WINS!** To build your PURPOSEFUL, PASSION-FILLED Personal Brand every day, you will stack wins and those stacked wins will add up to your BIG WINS overtime!

DECIDE. COMMIT. RESOLVE.

DECIDE. What One Decision WILL I MAKE Today That Will Create Wins In My Life?

> *"I will make the DECISION that I want to make my greatest impact and to do that I have decided to take action and implement the WIN ALL DAY Personal Branding Game plan!"*

COMMIT. What Am I Deciding Today That IS GOING TO HAPPEN in my life?

> *"I am deciding today to commit to be my best and create my Personal Brand. To do this I am committed to executing the WIN ALL DAY Personal Branding Game plan!"*

RESOLVE. What Am I Deciding Today that IS ALREADY DONE in my life?

> *"I am deciding that it is already done! That I will be the BEST version of me, I will create a new story for my life, I will live a life of purpose, significance, and true fulfillment so that I can make my greatest impact and walk out my calling and fulfill my destiny. It is already done!"*

YOUR BREAKTHROUGH IS COMING

I am not sure what motivated you to pick up this book at this time in your life but I BELIEVE that you did so on purpose. There are defining moments in time when we make certain decisions that have the possibility to change it all and I believe that this moment in time will be that for you. I am not sure what your life looks like at the moment but you are making a decision to want to be more and achieve more in life, and as you sow you shall reap!

As you make the decision, commit and operate with resolve by implementing the WIN ALL DAY Personal Brand Game plan, you are going to create and experience BREAKTHROUGHS in your life!

As my mentor Tony Robbins says,

"A BREAKTHROUGH IS THE MOMENT IN TIME WHEN THE IMPOSSIBLE BECOMES POSSIBLE."

Your Breakthrough Is Coming! Expect a Breakthrough in your personal and professional life as you go through this process of building your personal brand.

Personal Breakthroughs – Expect to create shifts in beliefs, perceptions, and standards.

Business Breakthrough – Expect to create strategies, ideas, systems, step-by-step game plans, and visions to make progress in your business.

WHAT DO YOU WANT?

"Write the vision and make it plain so that you can run with it."

The Bible: Habakkuk 2:2

Before we start this journey of you building your PURPOSE-driven, highly profitable Personal Brand I want to ask you two questions…

First, what is WINNING to you? Your "What" is your VISION. If you don't know what you want, you will never get it.

What does a WINNING life look like to you? What does WINNING in business look like for you?

What do you need to get out of life-long term? What do you need to get from your Personal Brand long term?

Where are you? Where do you want to be? Clarify the results you desire in life. A crystal-clear compelling vision for the future is needed to WIN! You will define that in this game plan, and as you go through this book each day your "WHAT" will become more crystal clear and your Vision will come to life!

WHAT IS YOUR "WHY"?

Second, WHY do you want to WIN? Your "WHY" is your PURPOSE. This is your driver and juice. Your motivator, the reason you do what you do! This is what pulls on you to overcome laziness, procrastination, worry, doubt, fear, and to not be led by emotions and feelings.

THE GREATEST FORCE IN LIFE... IS THE SOUL ON FIRE. A LIFE ON PURPOSE!

Why do you do what you do? Why do you have to have your "WHAT"? Think about the impact you could make. The quality of life you could have for you and your loved ones?

You have to make what's in front of you STRONGER
than what's behind you!

You have to make what's inside of you BIGGER
than what's outside of you!

You have to make what you want GREATER
than your greatest excuse!

CREATE YOUR NEW STORY

"The only thing keeping you from getting what you really want in life is THE STORY you keep telling yourself of why you don't or can't have it!"

Change your STORY. Change your life. Today is the day you stop making up stories to excuse the result you are getting at the moment.

"YOU only get a new result by taking a new action. You only take a new action by creating a NEW STORY!"

Your story is a series of beliefs that you create around something. Change your belief, change your life! **BELIEF** is a feeling of certainty about what something means. The meaning of anything in life ONLY has the meaning YOU choose to give it! What you look for, you will find! Start to assign your life, your business, and anything you desire in life a new meaning, give it a new story so that you can create a new belief.

Building your Personal Brand is going to be a life changing experience for you. Being able to do what you love, what you're PASSIONATE about, making an IMPACT, and PROFITING at the same time is awesome. But what you are really doing is creating a new story for your life.

"The true reward is the person you will become on the way to creating your new story!"

Most people never get what they want in life…or become who they were called to be because they are led by emotions and feelings. YOUR emotions no longer dictate and determine what you do. YOUR actions do. Throughout this game plan you will take action until you act your way into feeling.

Most people want to WIN and be successful but very few people are actually running the right plays to WIN. This is your game plan, the plays you need to run to create your personal brand so that you can create the life you desire and deserve to ultimately WIN.

"DO MY DAILY ACTIONS LINE UP WITH WHAT I SAY I WANT?"

MOTIVATION TO WIN

Motivation comes and goes. If you wait until you are motivated to take action you will never create your PURPOSE-DRIVEN PERSONAL BRAND and WIN ALL DAY. You see, what's wrong is always available and many times we lose motivation and get stuck managing our circumstances that we don't have time to create our life!

Short term motivation comes from getting a result! Long term motivation comes from short term momentum. Using this game plan will help you to bring back the motivation by stacking wins and creating momentum. As you build your personal brand you will produce these small wins each day, and over time when you see the impact that your story, your knowledge, your skillset, and your wisdom has on others, you will be motivated.

The WIN ALL DAY Personal Brand Proven Process

This book is broken down into four sections. Each section consists of chapters with the game plan for you to build your WINNING personal brand. This book is created in an action guide format, which means you have to do the work. In each chapter there are specific actions for you to take so that by the time you are done, you will have brought clarity to your WINNING personal brand.

Section one is, WHO?
Who are YOU? First, we will bring clarity to your brand per-

sonality. It all starts with **YOU**! You are the personal brand. Your gifts, your trials, and everything has led to this time in your life. It is all part of your story and why people need what you have. **YOU** are the brand, so to build a highly profitable business we have to first build **YOU**.

Who do you serve? Then we will discover **WHO you were called to serve.** Who your dream customer/client is and how you can identify and relate to them. And how to create the identity shift needed for them to buy.

During this phase we will also breakthrough any limiting beliefs, fears, and preconceived ideas that have been holding you back from **WINNING**.

Section two, WHAT?

In this section we will create your **VISION** for your life and your **Personal Brand** business. We will identify what your **PASSIONS** are in life and we will create your personal brand around what you **LOVE** to do. Your PASSIONS and your VISION are what will bring clarity to your business.

Through your Passion and your Vision, we will create your new reality.

Then we will create your **Market Niche** so that we know exactly who and where your **Dream Clients** are, along with their deepest problems and biggest desires that will be solved by your personal brand.

Lastly, we will create your **Irresistible Offer** to bring clarity to who you are, what you do, and how you do it. This will bring you direction and clarity in your marketing, selling, social media posting, and most of all peace of mind.

Section three, WHY?

Your **PURPOSE**. During this phase of building your highly profitable personal brand we will bring clarity around **what your PURPOSE is**. Both in life and in your Personal Brand.

We will work through the identity shift and why your personal brand is way bigger than just a business...It is a **MOVEMENT!**

We will breakdown how to create your movement and build your mission-based business around your personal brand while working with ONLY your **DREAM clients**; and how to turn these dream clients into raving fans and a part of your tribe!

This is what it's ALL about, making your greatest **IMPACT** in life, **SERVING** the people YOU were **CALLED** to serve and getting **PAID** to do it!

Section four, YOUR PLAYBOOK

This is when we now get into the strategy and tactical side of your personal branding business. This is where we take everything we did up until this point and put it all together.

You now are **THE AUTHORITY**. You are the **EXPERT**! We will choose your "BIG ONE" - the product/service that is going to complete your front-end offer, your flagship offer for your personal brand.

We will create your Brand Voice, Your Online Social Media Presence, and craft your plan on how to get your message out to your Dream clients.

Your blueprint, your game plan, your **PLAYBOOK**! These are your X's and O's and the plays you need to run to grow and scale. The goal now is to take everything we've built and bring it to **LIFE**.

You will have a step-by-step game plan for your Personal Branding Business that we just created on how to execute so that you can make your **VISION** a reality.

We will walk through your one year plan, your quarterly goals, your monthly targets, your weekly scoreboard, and your daily stacks so that you can produce WINS and create your dream life. You'll wake up everyday with PASSION, fueled by PURPOSE as you are serving your dream clients, making your greatest impact and income.

THAT IS WINNING ALL DAY!

"If You Want Something You've Never Had, You've Got To Do Something You've Never Done... and Do It Every Day!"

With this same game plan, I was able to build my personal brand, "Coach JC", which has led me to be able to make my greatest impact and do it as a business. Through the Coach JC personal brand I wrote 4 books and built 4 brands.

I started the first ever women's only fitness bootcamp in Tulsa Oklahoma with no money in the bank and just eight driven women. Bootcamp Tulsa has now been named one of The Top 10 Fitness Bootcamps in the entire nation.

Through my personal brand, I was able to open my dream sports performance facility, Dynamic Sports Development, and over the last 12 years have been fortunate and blessed to train some of the top athletes in the entire world.

I started my life coaching/performance business to help people overcome limiting beliefs and create breakthroughs in life. We do that through coaching, my podcast, and online courses. Because of building my personal brand by the age of 29, I was named Tulsa's Young Entrepreneur of the Year, was selected as one of Oklahoma's 30 under 30 Entrepreneurs, and was also selected as one of *Oklahoma's 40 under 40 Entrepreneurs.*

I launched my own supplement line, The WIN ALL DAY supplement line. I have been blessed to speak on some of the largest stages in the world and even opened up for the President of the United States, Donald J. Trump.

We launched our non-profit, Fit First Responders to serve those that serve us, the finest and bravest from our law enforcement, firefighters, medics and military.

Started our coaching and marketing company to help others with a story and a message to do the same and that is why you are reading this book today.

Is any of this luck? Heck no!

I tell you this because if I could do it – an Italian kid from the Jersey shore with no business or success background – then you can too!

This book is short, simple, and exactly what you need to know to build your personal brand. The game plan will not work for you unless you work it. This one book has the potential to absolutely TRANSFORM your life forever if you allow it to. Building a personal brand worked for me and it will work for you!

Are You Ready?

SECTION ONE: WHO
WHO ARE YOU? WHO DO YOU SERVE

LESSON ONE
WINNING MINDSET

You want to WIN?! Mindset is a huge part of you **WINNING**. Throughout this book we will spend a lot of time on MINDSET. For you to be YOUR BEST and live a purpose-driven life, conditioning your mindset is going to be a huge part!

You will train your mind just like you train your body!

I read a book, *Mindset* by Carol S. Dweck that is an absolute gamechanger! One of the main concepts from the book Mindset is that the view you adopt for yourself directly affects the way you live your life.

Carol digs deep into these two kinds of mindsets. We all have two mindsets and which mindset you choose to live in is the single biggest factor to what your life looks like. Your mindset can directly and significantly affect the direction of your life. For better or for worse!

You want to change your reality, change your mindset!

The two mindsets are: **The Fixed Mindset** and **The Growth Mindset.**

I started to study these different mindsets and break any belief of a fixed mindset and adopt a full out growth mindset.

Of course, because my brand is WIN ALL DAY, I labeled them, **The Losing Mindset** and **The WINNING Mindset!**

Do you view the world as a court with a jury, where you are constantly judged or as a playing field, playing your game, running your plays, constantly learning, growing, and winning?

The Losing (Fixed) Mindset is living with an urgency to prove yourself, fear of failure, and fear of judgement.

The WINNING (Growth) Mindset is living life with the mindset that everything is a growth opportunity; embrace failure and obstacles as opportunities, and overcome rejection and judgment.

Here is a great comparison of the two mindsets...

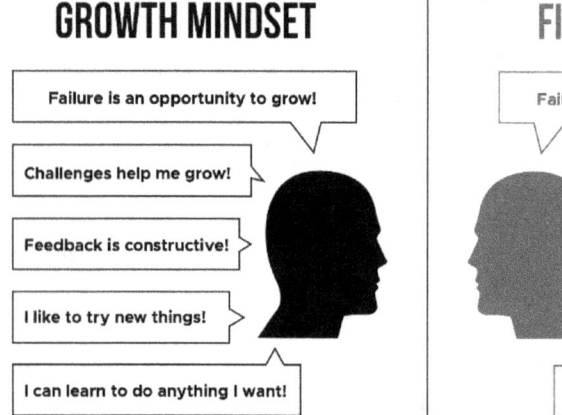
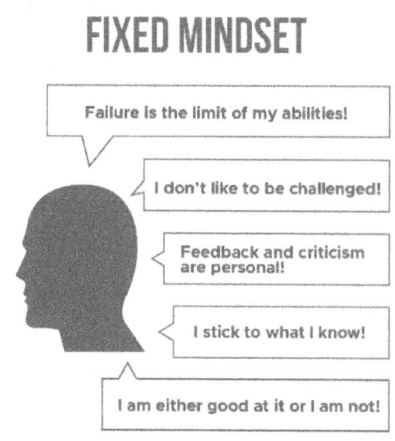

A person with a **Losing (fixed) mindset** believes their qualities, intelligence, and talents are fixed traits and cannot be changed. With this mindset there is no drive to work to develop and improve them.

A person with a **WINNING (growth) mindset** believes that their qualities, intelligence, and talents can grow so they are willing to put the time in to develop and gain this experience. A growth-minded person puts the effort in with a belief that their effort has a direct effect on their success.

People with a **losing mindset** avoid challenges, because they make them feel like they're not talented or smart. They lose interest when the work gets hard, and they give up easily. NOT YOU!

They let one setback... one bad test... obstacle...trail, storm, or outcome define their worth and life. NOT YOU!

People with **The WINNING Mindset** thrive on challenges and even seek them. They welcome getting uncomfortable to stretch themselves, because that brings growth and learning.

If you have a **WINNING mindset**, you choose to not let one single outcome define your ability or your potential. You look at the obstacle, trail, storm, and setbacks as a single point in time, and don't let them define you or what you are capable of in the future!

THE WINNING MINDSET

"I am committed and have to work hard to achieve success. I love what I am doing and trust the process regardless of the outcome! Each rep is meaningful and I CHOOSE to apply what I have and give my best, embracing challenges and welcoming the uncomfortable. I will stretch myself to grow, learn, develop, do more, be more, think bigger, and take more risks regardless of the outcome."

CREATE THE WINNING MINDSET

What Challenges Have I Avoided?

What Opportunities Have I Missed Out On?

What Challenge Will I Choose To Face Starting Immediately So I Can Create The Winning Mindset?

LESSON TWO
WHO ARE YOU?

ONE OF THE GREATEST BELIEFS YOU COULD HAVE IN LIFE IS A BELIEF IN YOU!

WHO YOU were born to be!
WHO YOU are!
WHO YOU can become!

THE #1 ENEMY OF SUCCESS? **SELF DOUBT!**

Low self-esteem leads to low self-image and causes us to not show up 100% who we are in life 100%. Self-esteem is how we view ourselves. How you view YOURSELF!

Self-image is how we believe the world views us. So if we have a low self-esteem we believe the world views us that same way. Because of this, we pull back, we retreat, we isolate, we say less and do less. We miss out and the world misses out on who we were called to be!

YOU were born with a purpose! YOU have a purpose. Throughout this course we are going to refine and define what that is.

BUT... It all starts with your identity!

There is no one like you! You were uniquely designed and created. You no longer have to be like that influencer on Instagram. You no longer have to try to be someone that your parents have wanted you to be.

Now is the time to be YOU, THE BEST version of YOU! The #1 chokehold of any person or business in growth and winning is **the psychology of the leader/ person.**

If you want to lead others you first have to lead yourself! Without confidence and self-esteem you will never make the impact you were called to make and that is why we start here!

THE #1 ENEMY OF SUCCESS? SELF DOUBT!

Every action originates with a thought.

What is your thought of YOU?
What is your belief of YOU?
What do you believe about yourself?

You see, it's not who you think you are in life that holds you back, it's who you think you're not.

You want to increase your winning percentage?
You want to win in business?!
You want to win in a relationship?!
You want to win in life?!

"DO NOT BE CONFORMED TO THE THINGS OF THIS WORLD, BUT BE TRANSFORMED BY THE RENEWING OF YOUR MIND."
ROMANS 12:2

Transform your mind! Just like you train your body, you can train your mind.

So let's train your mind, get your thoughts to line up with who you were born to be!

Let's bring back a belief in YOU and who you were created to be so that you can WIN and make your greatest impact and live a purpose-driven life!

Let's start with who you are NOT...

YOU ARE NOT...
Something negative that a teacher, a boss, or a parent told you at a young age.

YOU ARE NOT...
What has happened to you, the rejection, your past mistakes, limiting beliefs, or failures.

YOU ARE NOT...
What you do. Your career, and work does not define you. That's what you do, not who you are.

Your identity is not in what you do for a living, it's not in the success you have had, in the failures you have experienced, the mistakes you've made, your past, or what someone told you or said about you.

WHO ARE YOU...

In case you need a little help in getting started here you go...

You are a WINNER, WARRIOR, GLADIATOR, WORLD CHANGER. YOU ARE STRONG, POWERFUL, PASSIONATE, LOVING, CARING, COMPASSIONATE, CONFIDENT, SECURE, FREE, CREATIVE, DISCIPLINED, FUN, HAPPY, AND HEALTHY. YOU ARE A WINNER!

You see, when you come to a true understanding of who you are, you can then transform your mind and increase your impact and profit.

You see, your life is defined by your beliefs about who YOU are. If you want to transform your life, you need to change your identity. Creating a new identity is about creating a new belief.

The first step is to make a decision to dissociate yourself with your old identity (beliefs). Your old identity was formed over time and based around beliefs created by stories from situations and circumstances. Just like you can condition yourself to create new beliefs, at one point in time the same was done with negative beliefs that were nurtured and over time stories were created until they became a reality. These stories when negative have a negative impact on your life and your life is a reflection of these stories that all stem from your view of YOU!

Once you make a shift in your identity, your perception of yourself shifts and from there you can create your new reality.
So how do you make this shift in your identity?

MAKE A DECISION – You have to make a decision that you want to change your identity and do it NOW! You then have to make a decision of what new kind of identity you want to have moving forward. The decision that you will make is to replace that old identity of "I am not good enough!" with "I am more than enough!" You will make the decision on what your new belief is off of who you are and this is not based off of how you feel at the moment, what you have, or your false, old identity. Think of the areas of your life and who you want to be in these areas. Your fitness, your spiritual life, your finances, and your relationships.

Who are you?

Who do you need to be?

Who do you need to become?

LESSON THREE
DON'T ACCEPT FAILURE

"SUCCESS IS NOT FINAL; FAILURE IS NOT FATAL: IT IS THE COURAGE TO CONTINUE THAT COUNTS."
WINSTON CHURCHILL

Don't accept failure anymore! I don't care what happened in the past, and starting today, you don't care either. Failure is not an option. Today and from here on out, you will establish the no-quit mentality, the no-quit attitude.

The only way that you will ever fail is if you don't finish. There is no other way that you can fail if you have the RIGHT game plan, your daily action steps are executed, and you stick with it!

Now get focused on the prize and never quit! Start today and begin to allow your vision to expand! Here is the commitment that you will use to hold yourself accountable to sticking with it.

My Goal(s) is(are)...
1.

2.

3.

"I hereby state that I will abide by my goals listed above. This commitment is between me and me. I know that I can do it! I know that I will achieve them! Failure is not an option! I will not quit until I get there. There is no stopping me! I have the discipline, the determination, and the will to achieve all of my goals! From this day forward I consider it done! I will complete my goals by _____(date)."

Signature

Date

*Hang this in a visible place where you will see it every day and say it every day.

LESSON FOUR
NO MORE EXCUSES

"WHAT'S MORE IMPORTANT: YOUR EXCUSE OR WHAT YOU WANT?"
COACH JC

You will become successful today by no longer making excuses in your life. You know what they say about excuses!

It's time to take responsibility for YOU! It's your body, your career, your relationship, your life! This is such a powerful thing because without it you will look at your life as a failure, keep making excuses, and never accomplish your dreams and goals. Once you take responsibility, you will begin to experience peace and joy in your life and take full control over every situation. It's time to be honest with yourself. Starting today, eliminate words like "I can't," or "but" in your vocabulary! Stop talking yourself out of getting what you truly desire. What's more important: your excuse or your desire?

What can I do better?

How can I do more?

LESSON FIVE
LET NEGATIVITY GO

"DWELLING ON THE NEGATIVE SIMPLY CONTRIBUTES TO ITS POWER"
SHIRLEY MACLAINE

What negative influences in your life are holding you back from being a great success and accomplishing your goals?

Starting today, it's time to eliminate negativity from your life! You know what I'm talking about! It could be someone or something that you have allowed to beat you up so badly that it has kept you from what you want. You need to identify those negative things and start today to eliminate them from your life. Maybe you need to break some negative patterns or habits that you have created. These habits could include things you do, read, or watch – things that may be robbing you of your valuable time. Maybe it's someone in your life that has told you, "you can't do it," or maybe it's the environment that you are in on a daily basis that is holding you back. These negative forces in your life, both internal and external, will continue to drain you and hold you back from what you truly deserve. It all comes down to one word, my friend, CHOICE! Choose today to change the things you are doing, dissociate with negative people, change your environment, and do whatever you need to do to GET WHAT YOU DESERVE!

What negative things in my life have been holding me back and what will I replace them with starting today?

Negative habits?

Replace with

Negative Individuals?

Replace with

Negative Environment?

Replace with

LESSON SIX
DETERMINE YOUR ATTITUDE

"IF YOU DON'T LIKE SOMETHING, CHANGE IT; IF YOU CAN'T CHANGE IT, CHANGE THE WAY YOU THINK ABOUT IT."
MARY ENGELBREIT

You've heard it said, "Success starts with attitude." I believe they almost have it right. Your attitude is the second part in the success process and crucial to your success. It all starts with your thinking and your mindset about that success. Your THINKING is what ultimate creates your ATTITUDE, your attitude creates your ACTIONS, your actions will determine your RESULTS, and your results will ultimately dictate your success and what you get out of LIFE.

So why is your attitude so important? You got it! It's because your attitude directly determines your actions! Your attitude will make the difference in how you execute the daily action steps to get to your vision. Your attitude reflects who you are, and what is on the inside is what comes out. What kind of RESULTS do you want to get? What kind of LIFE do you want to live? Your attitude is a choice and starting today you will choose to bring the attitude that lines up with getting to what you desire.

Take Action!

My attitude starting today is

*I choose today and each and every day to choose my attitude so that it lines up with what I desire. I will no longer allow my feelings and situations to determine my attitude for me.

LESSON SEVEN
WHO DO I SERVE?

YOUR future clients NEED YOU! This is bigger than just a business. This is your PURPOSE! This is your CALLING! These are the people that you were called to help and serve.

The mindset shift that you will make starting today is:

"THESE PEOPLE NEED ME! THEY NEED WHAT I HAVE! I WAS CALLED TO THEM! THEY ARE STUCK AND I HAVE WHAT THEY NEED TO GET THEM UNSTUCK! MY MISSION IS TO SERVE THEM AND ADD SO MUCH VALUE TO THEIR LIFE!"

It's about creating a servant mindset. This perspective will change it all. When you make the shift from, "They are a customer" to "They are part of my calling and I am here to serve them!" You will show up differently and engage differently and when you serve unexpectedly you always get more back in return than what you give!

Here are some ways to help define this person:
- The person you used to be and were able to overcome – you now have a heart to help those people do the same.
- Something you hate and want to change in the world.
- Something you are passionate about and want to bring to people.
- Someone close to you that you love.
- Someone you could relate to from experiences, hobbies, traits, etc…

YOU ONLY NEED TO REACH YOUR PEOPLE.

YOU CAN NOT SERVE THE ENTIRE WORLD.

FOCUS ON YOUR PART OF THE WORLD, THAT YOU WERE CALLED TO SERVE.

THROUGH YOUR PURPOSE-DRIVEN BRAND YOU WILL MAKE A HUGE IMPACT THERE.

THOSE PEOPLE ARE WAITING FOR YOU TO SHOW UP.

So, let's get specific on who you serve, who you want to serve, and who you need to serve!

Who do I currently serve?

Who do I want to serve?

Who do I need to serve?

What do they love?

What do I like about them?

What do I love about them?

LESSON EIGHT
WHAT'S YOUR STORY

"YOU ARE WHO YOU ARE BECAUSE OF YOUR PAST CHOICES; WHO WILL YOU CHOOSE TO BE IN THE FUTURE?"
COACH JC

You have a past; I have a past; we all have a past! Your past can be your worst enemy or your biggest ally! You can allow your past to haunt you and hold you back from great success in business and in life, or you can use it to shape you to do great things and get what you deserve.

I have seen so many people who just could not let go of the past, and they allowed their past to control their future. I don't care what happened yesterday or 20 years ago, it's done! Why allow something that is now out of your control to control you? You may have failed in a business deal, you may not have lost all the weight you desired, or you may have had a bad game... Learn from it and move on, my friend! Don't allow these feelings of depression, guilt, or anxiety control your success. If you live in the past, you will not be able to fully live in the present or in the future. Why be controlled by something you cannot currently control? Starting today, you will use your past to create future successes.

I want you to think of a past situation that may be holding you back right now, and I want for you to ask yourself, what did I learn? You can take any situation, good or bad, and make it a learning experience. These past memories, good or bad, are a part of us. The key is to realize that they are not the reality of who you are right now and then use them to your advantage. So, what did you learn? Maybe something you could have done differently to get a different result, maybe put yourself into a different environment, or maybe it could have been how you reacted to the situation. What could you have done differently? What did you do wrong? What did you do right? I once heard it said, "A smart man learns from his own mistakes; a wise man learns from the mistakes of others!" Learn from it and allow it to propel you to greater success.

Not only will you learn from it but you will build your Personal Brand from it! This is YOUR personal brand! It is YOU! People want YOU! They want what YOU have! YOUR personality! Your mess you've been through! What you have been blessed to overcome! Your skillset! YOUR wisdom! YOUR idea! YOUR knowledge! YOUR purpose! YOUR mission! YOUR vision! And all of that is YOUR STORY!

One of the most important elements and one of the scariest parts for many when building a personal brand is putting your STORY into the world!

Your brand story is you being vulnerable and the thing that will make you relatable. Your brand story is the ONE thing that separates you from everyone else in your market. It's YOUR story and no one else has YOUR story! Where you come from, what you've been through, how you got here, today!

Build Your Brand Story

What past situation or challenges have you overcome?

What have you learned from these situations?

How can these things that you have overcome help other people WIN in life?

SECTION TWO: WHAT

CREATE YOUR VISION. CREATE YOUR OFFER.

LESSON NINE
WINNING STARTS WITH DESIRE

"TO GET WHAT YOU WANT IN LIFE YOU MUST FIRST MAKE A VERY IMPORTANT CHOICE...YOU MUST DECIDE WHAT IT IS YOU WANT!"
COACH JC

What is it that you really want? If you don't know what you want you will never get it! It all starts with desire! You Must Want It! You must have a desire to achieve, do more and to ultimately WIN! So, what is that thing that you may have wished for or hoped for; that thing that you may have been dreaming about? Maybe it's to make more money, create more time freedom, make a greater impact, write a book, or start a podcast.

If you don't know what it is, you'll never get it! This is the big picture, the thing you dream of, your ultimate life. What does that look like to you? Building your Personal Brand is about you doing what you love and making money doing it. It's about you making a great impact and being highly profitable at the same time. It's also about you creating a lifestyle so that you can live the ultimate life, the life you were born to live.

We all have those things that we want to get or achieve, but so many times it's just about refining it to know exactly what it is. You have to be specific about it. If you don't know where you want to go, you'll never get there. This is so important because what you desire is where your focus will go. Once you know what it is that you desire you must then place a timeline on it. What date will you accomplish this desire?

What is it that I really want in building my Purpose-driven, Passion-filled life?

What is it that I really want in building my Personal Brand?

How much do I really desire this?

When do I desire this by?

LESSON TEN
CHANGE YOUR THINKING

"CHANGE YOUR THINKING, CHANGE YOUR RESULTS"

You can have anything you want, any time you want it, once you create the winning mindset. It all starts in the head, my friend. You are truly only six inches away from getting what you want. It's the six inches from your left ear to your right ear: YOUR MINDSET!

THE WINNING MINDSET

I want you to think about this for a second....
What is that thing you truly desire: Your "WHAT", that burning desire that you identified in the last chapter? Okay, now going off of my "Create the Winning Mindset System" from above, I

want you to envision that exact thing where it says LIFE. Check out how simple this really is. Just work your way backwards and ask yourself:

1. What RESULTS do I need to get to that thing I truly desire?
2. What ACTIONS do I need take to get me those results?
3. What ATTITUDE do I need to bring everyday so my actions line up with what I say I want?
4. What am I THINKING, what's my MINDSET?! It all starts right there. Success or failure isn't some big event, my friend. It all comes down to how you think about it. It all starts in your head.

So many times we allow others to determine and dictate how we think about ourselves. Over time, these beliefs become a lid on our life to keep us from great success. The power of the mind is incredible! These "limiting beliefs" or "mental barriers" are real and are a lot more powerful than people believe them to be. Starting today, you must not believe what others – the media, your family members, magazines, other books, co-workers, social media comments, etc. – are saying. It is time to take the lid off of your life and start to break some records. It is time to think big! Change your thinking and you will change your results!

What thoughts have been holding you back from WINNING?

*Choose today to let go of this kind of thinking! Remove the negative thinking, and make a decision on a daily basis to break through your mental barriers and live the life You Were Born to Live!

LESSON ELEVEN
MY PASSION IS

"YOU CAN DO WHAT YOU LOVE AND LOVE WHAT YOU DO!"

You might be starting from the beginning and have no idea what you are passionate about…or you may have been through many life experiences and have a great idea of what your passions are.

Your passion can be a variety of things and that is ok, but as we build your personal brand the goal is to be able to take your gifts, talents, abilities, and what you are passionate about and make money doing it as a business.

A passion is something that you associate with a massive amount of pleasure. Something that you think of and makes you excited and happy.

To find your passion you have to try stuff, you have to experience things. You have to be willing to get out of your comfort zone so that you can experience new things and try out opportunities until you find what you are passionate about.

This doesn't mean you are going to be great immediately at everything you try. It doesn't mean you are going to love every part of the process even when you are passionate about one thing.

Let me give you a little insider… every job sucks sometimes. There's no such thing as some passionate career where you will never get tired, burnt out, and stressed over. That's some fancy marketing hype or some fantasy, so stop believing it. I am living

my dream job (which is my purpose and mission), and I still don't enjoy every part of everything I have to do to make it a reality.
My point is that each step leads to the next step in finding out what you are truly passionate about! Some things worked out well, others not so much, some things I was more excited about than others, some I became passionate about once I became good at them.

But each one was an important step for me to discover what my passion was and what it wasn't.

Bring clarity to your passion in four simple questions:

What Skillsets Have I Developed:
(you have developed over the years):

What Knowledge Have I Acquired:
(all that you have gained):

What Obstacles Have I Overcome:
(any you have overcome):

What Do I love to do:
(what lights you up)

LESSON TWELVE
DON'T FEAR FAILURE

"MOST OF THE THINGS I HAVE ACCOMPLISHED IN LIFE HAVE BEEN OUT OF THE FEAR OF BEING MEDIOCRE."
COACH JC

Think about it... How many times have you passed up an opportunity because you were scared of failing? Maybe you were scared of rejection, hearing no, or perhaps, that you just may not be able to do it. Fear can keep you from relationships, career opportunities, losing weight, greater performance, and ultimate happiness and success. Fear can keep you from building your Personal Brand! Fear can keep you from making your greatest impact and income. I've been there! Fear can paralyze you right where you're at and can become your worst enemy if you allow it to.

I want to ask you a question: What are you really afraid of? Are you scared that you won't succeed? Are you scared that you may not make the impact you desire? Are you fearful that you experience rejection and judgment? Who cares?! This fear can torture you if you don't take control of it now. This fear will prevent you from achieving ultimate success and WINNING. Think about how many times in your past you knew that you could have done something but did not act on it because of fear of failure. Really, think about it, what is the worst that could happen?

Did you know that you were only born with two fears? That's right! You were only born with the fear of falling and the fear of loud noises. This is great news for you because that means that all other fears have been created, and if you created them, then you can overcome them!

Where does this fear of failing come from? You got it: the same place it all starts, in your THINKING! You cannot allow fear of failure to be part of your thinking, and then allow it to determine your attitude and actions on a daily basis. Instead, you will start to attack these situations in life! Overcoming fear is a two-step process.

First, you must detect what this fear is in your life, and second, you must TAKE ACTION on it!

What has fear kept me from achieving in my life?

What action am I going to take today to overcome this fear in my life?

LESSON THIRTEEN
KNOWLEDGE IS POWER

"KNOWLEDGE IS LIKE A GARDEN: IF IT IS NOT CULTIVATED, IT CANNOT BE HARVESTED."
AFRICAN PROVERB

You've heard it before...People perish for the lack of knowledge! I say it a little differently: "People perish for the lack of the RIGHT Knowledge!" With so much information out there it's easy to get overwhelmed and overloaded. You have the game plan in your hands to build your Personal Brand. Often people feel inadequate or not qualified to build their Personal Brand and this leads to fear. One of the greatest ways to breakthrough this limiting belief is to become the expert. To know your stuff!

I want you to ask yourself some questions, "What do I know?" "What is the knowledge I have?" "What have I done that I could teach others to do?" Now I want you to think about what you really need to know to get you what you want. What do you need to do today to get the RIGHT information, to gain the RIGHT knowledge to be the expert so that you can have confidence in what you do? You will always be a student and constantly be learning, but starting today, you will stay focused on the RIGHT information. Forget about everything else, my friend; knowledge is power, and people will pay you for your knowledge!

What are you really good at? What are you great at? Maybe you already have a set of skills or maybe you are in the process of acquiring those skills. What Have I Done? What have you studied and mastered? What do I love that I need to learn more about?

This is not about faking it until you make it. It is about having a skill, that you can provide value through, in exchange for compensation.

You have to make the INVESTMENT! The investment in TIME. ENERGY. EFFORT.

Take what you are passionate about and if you aren't already GREAT at it, then GET GREAT at it! As you get great at it you will become even more passionate about it! Go deep in becoming THE BEST at it! Not good! Not average! THE BEST!

What knowledge do I have that people need/want?

What skillsets do I need to improve on to grow my Personal Brand?

How will I further this knowledge and develop my skillset?

By when will I have this knowledge?

LESSON FOURTEEN
THINK BIG

"BELOVED, I PRAY THAT IN ALL RESPECTS YOU MAY PROSPER AND BE IN GOOD HEALTH, JUST AS YOUR SOUL PROSPERS."
3 JOHN 2

Now it's time for you to THINK BIG! I have had the privilege to train and work with some of the top athletes in the world at our sports performance facility, Dynamic Sports Development, in Tulsa, Oklahoma. A lot of the athletes that we train have big dreams. It's awesome to see how big they dream; to be great in their individual sports and hopefully play at the next level. When you are doing the necessary things and executing the daily action steps, then you should expect big things.

What you expect from yourself is what you will get, and what you expect from yourself is what others will expect out of you. Just like these athletes, you now have the right game plan and are executing the daily rituals so you should expect big things and big results! Don't accept being average or mediocre. Do all you do in excellence! Think Big and Act even Bigger!

You must change your thinking before you can ever make your greatest impact. You must believe you can create wealth before you ever do. You must believe you can play at the highest level as an expert and deliver life changing results for your clients. You have to mentally build your Personal Brand before you ever build it. You have to see yourself teaching what you know to others and through you and your knowledge while changing lives. You have to see yourself getting compensated to do so. You have to see you and your family living that dream life before you live it.

Don't limit yourself by where you currently are or by what you currently have. You have so much more potential than you even believe you do, my friend! If you don't believe in yourself, why should anyone else?

When you start to Think Big and stay focused on the end result, you will find ways to make things happen so that you get what you so badly desire. I'm not talking about hoping or wishing; I'm talking about calling it now as what it WILL be! The lives you will impact! The life you will create! The financial freedom you will experience! The legacy you will leave!

Today you will create your personal "I WILL" statement. This statement will be a powerful paragraph about those two or three things that you desire. No longer hoping, wishing, or wanting but rather claiming with "I WILL". You will then place this statement in three different visible areas so that each day you can remind yourself of what you WILL have. Your goal is to say this statement with authority and actually believe it each time you see it throughout the day. Be specific and vivid, and determine a specific date by which you WILL accomplish this goal.

I will...

LESSON FIFTEEN
THE BIG 3

HEALTH. WEALTH. RELATIONSHIPS.

These are "The Big 3". These are the Big 3 markets; when it comes to marketing, every product or service runs through one of these three. This is not something I came up with and think is just a cool idea. This is also not a suggestion. This is what years of marketing, market research, and all the experts have proven over time.

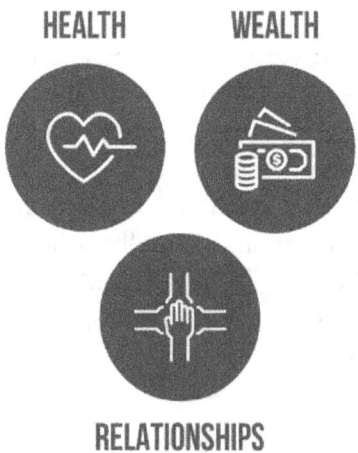

These Big 3 are the Big 3 areas that people, consumers are looking to buy something in that will bring them improvement or change. These 3 markets are where people are hoping for a specific result to achieve in their life.

As you build your brand, what you teach others, your skillset, your knowledge, your product or service MUST fit into one of these three markets for you to set yourself up to WIN. Your product/service MUST fit into one of The Big 3 and your message and marketing MUST fit into one of The Big 3.

The Big Questions for You to WIN

In which one of The Big 3 markets will my personal brand serve people in?

In which of The Big 3 is my Dream customer wanting to receive a result in?

In which of the Big 3 is my Dream customer ALREADY buying products or services in?

LESSON SIXTEEN
THROW THE LID OFF

"YOU CAN HAVE ANYTHING YOU WANT, ANY TIME YOU WANT IT, ONCE YOU CHANGE YOUR THINKING!"
COACH JC

It was May 6, 1954, and no runner competing in track and field had ever run a mile in less than four minutes. All the so-called experts and commentators declared that it would never be done. Studies were performed to show that it was not humanly possible and that no one could possibly run that fast for that long in order to make it happen. For years those tests and studies stood true, and no one broke the four-minute mile barrier. However, on that day in 1954, a man named Roger Bannister made sports history and ran a mile in 3 minutes and 59 seconds! Up until that point, the runners had allowed the opinions of others dictate their outcome. Roger Bannister trained hard and did not believe what all the experts were saying. He did not believe that it was impossible. He refused to let others determine his outcome, and he believed that he would break that four-minute mile run. He did not allow others to put a limit on his life. He was going to determine his own future and his own destiny.

This story is so fascinating not only because Roger Bannister made history but also because of what I am about to tell you: just 46 days later, another runner broke his record. Now, after more than 50 years, hundreds of runners have run a mile in less than four minutes! I want you to think about that. For hundreds of years no one could run the mile in less than four minutes. It was pretty much accepted that no man could break the four-minute mile barrier. It was believed that the four-minute mile was physically impossible. It was commonly accepted as a fact! However, the reality was that the four-minute mile was a psychological barrier!

So what happened? I will tell you. For all those years, athletes allowed others to set that barrier in their minds. For all those years runners believed what others said. Everyone was convinced that it was impossible. The lid was put on their abilities. The power of the mind is incredible! These "limiting beliefs" or "mental barriers" are real and are a lot more powerful than people believe them to be.

I am here to tell you that you can't believe what others are saying and most importantly you can't believe the lies you are telling yourself.

As you worked through the BIG 3 in the last chapter I know that there were questions that came up, like "How can I compete in the health market?" or "There are so many big names in the wealth market!" It is time to start to break some records. It is time to think big! Change your thinking and you will change your results. It's time to throw the lids off of your life and go crush your market and serve your people that you were called to serve.

What is your "four-minute mile" barrier?

What thoughts have been holding you back from WINNING?

Choose today to let go of this kind of thinking!

LESSON SEVENTEEN
YOUR IRRESISTABLE OFFER

Now it is time to create your **IRRESISTABLE OFFER.** I was first introduced to offers in marketing years ago but never really came to a true understanding of the power of them until I became part of Russell Brunson's group. There is no one better at breaking down an irresistible offer than Russell.

Your offer is your one liner, to your one sentence, to your paragraph elevator pitch that sums up who you help and how you help them. It is the thing that piques their interest. It has them wanting and needing more.

When someone asks you what you do, your irresistible offer will be your answer **EVERYTIME**! We will then, later, take your offer and create your "stack". Your stack is how you deliver on this offer.

As you continue to grow your personal brand your offer will evolve, you may have multiple offers and you may even have offers in different markets. The goal right now is to get one concrete offer, around your purpose and passion of what you love to do, that builds your personal brand business so that you can profit and highly profit.

LET'S CREATE YOUR IRRESISTABLE OFFER!

THE WHO (YOUR DREAM CLIENT)
Who is your target market? Who do you serve? This is your avatar, your dream customer/client that you already created.

THE WHAT
What is the pleasure they desire? What is the result they will get? What is their biggest problem? The pain they want to stop?

THE HOW
What is the process that you will take them through to get them the result? (This is your product or service, your expertise, skillset, knowledge)

Coach JC Example: "I Help/Coach (Entrepreneurs) To (Create Purpose-Driven, Highly Profitable Personal Brands) so they can turn their passion into profits and make their greatest impact while living a fulfilled life!" We do this by our online 6-week branding bootcamp through coaching and our proven 5 step system!"

SECTION THREE: WHY

**DISCOVER YOUR PURPOSE.
CREATE YOUR MOVEMENT.**

LESSON EIGHTEEN
KNOW YOUR PURPOSE

"CHERISH YOUR VISIONS AND YOUR DREAMS AS THEY ARE THE BLUEPRINTS OF YOUR ULTIMATE ACHIEVEMENTS."
NAPOLEON HILL

Why do you want that thing that you want? Why do you want to live that life of ultimate happiness, impact, and fulfilment? Why do you want to build your Personal Brand? Why do you want to teach what you know, your expertise, knowledge, and wisdom to help other people?

You have to know what it is you want, and you have to determine why you want this. This is your PURPOSE: the burning desire of why you have to have it. Your purpose is what will drive you, what is going to keep you motivated, and what is going to make your dream, your desire, become a reality. This is your burning passion to make that desire a reality. This is the reason for why you do what you do. This is the thing that you will stay focused on: the end result!

For you to truly succeed, you must know your reason why. This reason has to be specific and vivid!

Why do I really want to build my Personal Brand? Why do I want to make this impact?

Why do I want to create this lifestyle for me and my family?

How bad do I want/need this?

LESSON NINETEEN
GET BACK IN THE GAME

"FOR A RACE TO BE FINISHED, YOU MUST FIRST START."

I am a big fan of finishing and never quitting...You can't win a race if you don't finish, right?

Ask any runner and they will tell you that it's not about how you start but how you finish. That is true, but how will you ever finish if you don't start? You can't win the game if you are on the bench or in the locker room. Are you in the game? So many times, in life we drop out of our race, we put ourselves on the bench and never get the chance to see the prize at the finish line. Have you been knocked out of the race? Have you dropped out of the game?

If things don't start right, you can't just give up, you have to keep playing. Maybe you have tried to start a business before, maybe you have tried to discover your purpose, maybe you have hired a coach to help you find your passion, but you didn't see results, so you dropped out of the race. Maybe you hit a roadblock in life, financially, physically, or maybe even in a relationship. Did you know that Michael Jordan was cut from his high school basketball team? That's right, the greatest basketball player of all time didn't even make the team and it didn't stop him. Did you know that a guy named Walt Disney was told at his first trade show that he wasn't creative enough? That's right, look at him today. Disney World is one of the world's greatest vacation destinations. So, what's your excuse? You don't have one!

Today, I want you to get back into the game. Maybe this book is the starting point for you to lace em back up. To leave the locker room, to get off the bench. You aren't a spectator any longer. This is your life! Check yourself back in the game, baby. I don't care what has happened in the past, your new season begins today. Today is the day you get back on the court, the field, in the race– the race of your life. Think of every day of your life as just one lap in the competition of your race. Once that lap is over you will never get it back, and once the race is over, it's over. Life is short and once it's over, it's over. There is not another race. That thing you desire is at the finish line, but how badly do you want it?

Today, I want you to re-submit your name, put your sneakers on, and get back into the game. Once you get back in, then you will have a chance to win baby. You must refuse to be knocked down; you must refuse to be knocked out. Keep running, my friend, don't look back, stay focused on the end result...that finish line! This book was created to not only guide you through building your Personal Brand, but also to get you back into the game and together we will make it all the way to the finish line, your championship, your Super Bowl!

What do I need to do today to get back in the race, my game?

What do I see at the finish line?

LESSON TWENTY
OBSTACLES CREATE OPPORTUNITY

"DON'T LET OBSTACLES STOP YOU. IF YOU RUN INTO A WALL, DON'T TURN AROUND AND GIVE UP, FIGURE OUT HOW TO CLIMB IT, GO THROUGH IT, OR WORK YOUR WAY AROUND IT."

Are you ready? You had better be! Obstacles are going to occur, times are going to get tough, the road will be rocky, adversity will arise, and uncomfortable times will happen. This is a guarantee, my friend. The question is not, will it ever happen? Instead, the question is: what are you going to do when these inevitable circumstances occur? Starting today, you need to shift your perspective. Perspective can be the absolute game changer in your life. Obstacles are going to come; that's why the key is preparing for them now. How will you react? You will react by being proactive and shifting your perspective.

Circumstances happen, both good and bad. Some you can control, and others you just can't control. The name of the game is to prepare now so you don't react but rather act in order to flip the obstacle into an opportunity. How you react will determine the outcome.

For you to build your Personal Brand, make your greatest impact and turn it into your business so that you can do what you're PASSIONATE about and in order to walk out your PURPOSE, you MUST shift your perspective.

Your perspective, starting today is, no longer, "Why did this happen to me?" but rather, "This happened for me!" Your perspective is, "With every obstacle comes an equal or greater opportunity to WIN!"

What are you going to do when obstacles come at you? Flip it! You have to do whatever it takes to not let them stop you. Nothing can stop you! I don't care if you have to go through, around, over, or under. Whatever you have to do you must do it. This is something that is developed; shifting your perspective can be trained just like you train your body. You must make a conscious effort on a daily basis to fight through obstacles and not react based on how you feel but rather in the way that will get you the outcome you desire. Every day a situation will arise that will make you uncomfortable, so practice shifting your perspective. Use daily circumstances to make yourself better so that when the large obstacles are thrown at you, you will know how to respond.

Starting today I want you to learn how to flip obstacles into opportunity.

What is my perspective, that I will choose, when obstacles present themselves?

What are some examples in my life that were an obstacle but if my perspective was different, I could've flipped them into opportunity?

LESSON TWENTY-ONE
TAKE BACK THE POWER

"FIRST WE MAKE OUR HABITS; THEN OUR HABITS MAKE US."
CHARLES C. NOBLE

Your future is in your hands. You control your future, and you determine what happens now, tomorrow, and forever. You are where you are today because of the decisions you made yesterday. You will be who you are in the future based on the decisions you make today. I talk to so many people who have allowed other people and other people's situations to determine where they are currently. It's time you take responsibility for your actions. No one forces you to do what you do and no one forces you not to do it. You are in complete control of your life, and now by lining up your daily rituals you can change your life forever.

You are at this point in your life today because of the choices that you made yesterday. You control your future, and you control your life. TAKE BACK THE POWER. It's your life! Take control of it!

This is why your desire must be strong; it must be strong enough to overcome mental laziness. Some people want the easy way out because they have allowed their mental laziness to create an attitude of laziness, which has produced daily laziness in their actions. NOT YOU! Do not allow mental laziness to determine your future. Do not allow blaming to create your reality. You have to make a choice to no longer blame others for where you are at in life and to no longer complain about what you don't have. You must make the choice to overcome mental laziness. You control it, my friend! Stop settling because it's comfortable or easy at the moment.

Are you sacrificing what you want most in life for what you want at the moment?

You know what you want! Is what you want at the moment more important than getting what you want most in life? Do you really want to build this Personal Brand? Do you really want to make this impact? Do you really want to make that extra $50,000, $100,000.00 or even million a year? It's your choice, you control the outcome.

What areas of my life have I been allowing others to control?

What areas of my life do I need to take back the power, by taking responsibility?

LESSON TWENTY-TWO
BUILD A MOVEMENT

BUILD A MOVEMENT. My goal was always to create a movement that changed people's lives! And I believe you can do the same no matter what your Purpose-Driven Personal Brand is. People have built movements, companies have built movements, and there are both positive and negative movements. There are religious movements, political movements, and movements in every feasible way within The Big 3 Markets of Health, Wealth, and Relationships.

Every movement has a leader, and that is you! They have an opportunity for the people they are called to serve, and that's your offer!

How cool would it be to not just create a Personal Brand but to create lasting change through your brand? A brand that not only makes you money, but you create a movement around what you love doing and you change lives for the better forever!

This is when customer and clients become your greatest marketing as raving fans with big mouths, shouting your name and brand from rooftops. You build a following, a tribe, and repeat clients/customers that are loyal and lifetime family members of your brand.

You do this by giving them ownership. This is the I AM statement that gives them something to take ownership of. Anytime you put the words "I AM..." in front of something it gives a feeling of ownership. What is your tribe called, what do you refer to them as? This is the word you will play off of for naming certain programs, products, services and it is the term they will use to identify themselves with your brand.

What is my tribe's "I AM..." statement that will give them ownership within my movement?

Coach JC's WIN ALL DAY Ex. "I AM A WINNER!"

LESSON TWENTY-THREE
NEVER QUIT

"QUITTING IS LOSING, AND LOSING ISN'T WINNING!"

The one type of person who has always bothered me is the quitter. I cannot stand to see someone just quit and give up! Still to this day, it angers me. This "quitter mentality" can absolutely prevent you from accomplishing what you really want in life. It breaks my heart to know that so many times in life people are so close to their breakthrough right when they give up. Over the last few years in my life coaching business, I have discovered the reason why most people give up.

Most people quit because they feel as if they don't have the ability to accomplish what they want. Well, I have GREAT news for you! Did you know that your ability is only 5% responsible for you getting what you truly desire? ONLY 5%! So, what's the other 95%, you ask? For you to get the results you desire, create wealth, make your greatest impact, and build your Personal Brand, it all comes down to one word: STICKABILITY!
That's my fancy way of saying not quitting! Many people have a problem with following through until the end and giving up right before they are about to experience a giant breakthrough. Ninety-five percent of getting what you really want in life is just sticking with it, never quitting, grinding it out!

This is so important and can separate you once and for all from your competition. You need to establish a no-quit mentality – a no-quit attitude – so that you can get something you've never had. The key here comes down to the simple, small, daily action steps that you need to be taking each and every day to execute your game plan. It can't just be when you feel like it or when it's comfortable. You have to make the time and then stick with it until you get what you want!

What have I started that I have given up on?

What am I focused on right now that I will never quit at until I get it?

LESSON TWENTY-FOUR
EXPECT RESULTS

"IF YOU DON'T BELIEVE IN YOURSELF, WHY SHOULD ANYONE ELSE BELIEVE IN YOU?"

Expect Results! Preparation time is never wasted time, my friend, and if you are doing the things necessary to get what you desire, then you should expect results. The ones who are disciplined and who put the time into training and preparing should expect good things. They should expect results. Once you start to implement the program and implement it to the fullest, then you should expect to see the results you desire.

The mind is a powerful weapon. If you don't believe in yourself, then why should anyone else believe in you? I am not talking about being cocky and arrogant. I am talking about confidence, a confidence that you are taking care of business, that you are back in the race, and that you are not going to quit until you reach your final goal. The only one who can take you out of the game is yourself. While you are on the field you can't be defeated, while you are on the court you can't lose, while you are in the race you are the best on the track. Remember the only one who can take you out of the race is you!

Start expecting results, start expecting good things, and start expecting your life to take a turn in the right direction! The time of doubting yourself is over! Expect great things in your life, and expect that you will see the results you desire. Have confidence that you can do it. Expect to make a great impact! Expect to make more money! Expect to build your dream life! **Expect to get what you came for!** Expect results knowing that you are doing what is right. Expect results now that you are taking the risks needed to take control of your life. You now have the game plan that you need in order to do it. You have committed to finish the race and you are focused on the end result. Now is the time to expect results; never doubt that you can do it! Start to THINK, ACT, and FEEL as if you are already there. See It, Believe It, and Expect It to come to pass.

I believe in you! Believe in yourself!

What do I expect?

When do I expect this by?

LESSON TWENTY-FIVE
PRIORITIES

"YOU CAN ALWAYS TELL WHAT SOMEONE REALLY WANTS IN LIFE BY LOOKING AT THEIR PRIORITIES."

What are your priorities? Do you know why a lot of people dream of building a profitable personal brand but never do? Do you know why so many people wish to make money and never make it? Why so many people dream of making an impact on a large scale but never do? It's simple... It's because doing the daily action steps to get them to their goal was never made a priority. What is it that you really value in life? You can always tell a person's desires and values by their priorities. What are your priorities?

Now is the time to address the priorities in your life! I'm not talking about what you may say your priorities are but rather what your actions really reflect. Your priorities are not expressed by what you say; instead they are determined by your daily actions. It's the follow through or the action that is slowing down your progress. Starting today, you will need to make sure that what you ultimately want becomes a priority in your daily action steps.

Coach JC's Five Steps to Prioritize Your Priorities:
1. Know what you want – don't waiver from it.
   What Do I want?

2. Write it out – Make it clear and be specific and realistic.
   What are my Top 5 Priorities in getting what I want?

3. Live it out – Walk it out on a daily basis. Be who you say you are!
   Who am I?

4. Associate Yourself – Surround yourself with people who have similar priorities.
   Who will I surround myself with?

5. Give it a check-up – Re-evaluate your priority list on a weekly or monthly basis.
   When will my scheduled check-up be each week/month?

Now, stop talking about it and go and get it!

SECTION FOUR: YOUR PLAYBOOK
MAKE IT A REALITY.

LESSON TWENTY-SIX
WHAT'S YOUR GAMEPLAN

"I VISUALIZED WHERE I WANTED TO BE, WHAT KIND OF PLAYER I WANTED TO BECOME. I KNEW EXACTLY WHERE I WANTED TO GO, AND I FOCUSED ON GETTING THERE."
MICHAEL JORDAN

Do you have a Game Plan? All successful people have a plan of action! What's yours? What's your game plan that you will execute to get you to where you need/want to be? Execute the game plan that is in your hands right now so that you can get what you desire and deserve in walking out your Personal Brand.

Now, I want you to put together your own game plan, specific to that thing you desire. A game plan is what I need to do, the things I need to execute so that I can WIN. What are you going to work on, specific to the previous chapters so that you can set your Personal Brand up to WIN?

Today, develop your personal game plan. This should be a concrete action plan of the necessary components you will utilize to get what you want in building your Personal Brand.

What's my Gameplan?
(What are the things that need to happen?)

LESSON TWENTY-SEVEN
TAKE ACTION

"A REAL DECISION IS MEASURED BY THE FACT THAT YOU'VE TAKEN A NEW ACTION. IF THERE'S NO ACTION, YOU HAVEN'T TRULY DECIDED."
TONY ROBBINS

Now that you have developed your game plan, it's time to take action! What are your daily action steps to execute your game plan? What is that one, simple, disciplined thing that you will do each and every day to get where you need to be? This is called the Law of WINNING. Time can work for you or against you. This is the step when most people fail in the road to success. Most people know what they want, but very few people's daily actions line up with what they truly desire.

This is your game plan broken up into daily action steps. This is how you are going to follow the game plan to get what it is you truly desire. You have to be very specific here. These action steps answer what, when, where, and how. Be as specific as possible by listing exact times, locations, and step-by step-approaches that you will take to get it done. This written itinerary of when, where, and how you will do each daily component will transform your life forever. If you want something you've never had, you've got to do something you've never done.

List each area of your game plan and then list the daily action step that you will do to execute the game plan. (What, When, Where, How)

My daily action step for_____
is

LESSON TWENTY-EIGHT
ARE YOU ACCOUNTABLE?

"ACCOUNTABILITY IS MAKING THE DECISION TO ALLOW OTHERS TO MAKE YOU GREAT!"

You will only go as far as you are accountable! How are you holding yourself accountable? Who are you allowing to hold you accountable? So many people get uncomfortable when they hear the word accountability. Being accountable is a great thing and a must for you to reach your goals and get what you desire! Look at almost every successful person in life and you will find that they had true accountability throughout the process in achieving that success. It will not be easy for you to get what you desire. Tough times will occur, obstacles will arise, and adversity will come at you; this is when that accountability will be able to pull you through. You have to get accountable!

There will be times when you may not feel like executing your daily actions steps. So what do you do? YOU JUST DO IT! That's right! If you want something you've never had, you can't go by how you feel, my friend! It will be nice to have that accountability in place to remind you of why you do what you do and to keep you focused on your goal.

This does not mean that I am telling you to trust everyone and anyone. What I am telling you is to find someone who you trust and respect and allow them to make you better. This is someone who wants to see you achieve your goals and live your life to the fullest. No one cares about you getting what you truly desire as much as you, but this person or people may come in a second close to seeing you succeed. This is someone who you can be totally open, honest, and vulnerable with at all times.

Accountability is simple if you're willing to be held accountable. If you think you have arrived or want to let your pride stand in the way, then this may not be that simple for you. Here's how it works: you will tell this person your goals and the game plan that you will use to get that thing you desire. Then you will fill them in on what you think is going to be the most difficult part of the process for you. This is where you will ask them to help keep you motivated and focused on the prize and not to let you quit. You will ask them to hold you accountable to your weaknesses and make sure that you are executing your daily action steps. Iron sharpens iron! Who are you going to allow to sharpen you? Who are you sharpening?

How will you start today to be accountable to yourself?

Who will I contact today to allow to hold me accountable as I launch my Personal Brand?

LESSON TWENTY-NINE
SENSE OF URGENCY

"WITHOUT A SENSE OF URGENCY, DESIRE LOSES ITS VALUE."
JIM ROHN

Do you have a sense of urgency? How badly do you want to build this brand? How badly do you want to take control of your finances? How badly do you want to create more wealth, have a greater impact, be successful and WIN?

Those people who make things happen in life are those that possess a sense of urgency. A sense of urgency is established when something is of great importance to you, it is a necessity. You have got to have it. A lot of times this sense of urgency can bring some pressure, but if you want to do anything worthwhile, you had better learn to appreciate a little pressure. Pressure demands that you get it done. Pressure is knowing that when you wake up in the morning you must find a way to make it happen. Pressure is lying down at night and creatively thinking of ways to make it happen. Starting today, you need to feel that accomplishing your desire is a matter of life and death.

In my own life, a lot of the things I accomplished were due to the fact that I had a sense of urgency – I had to have or needed that thing. I distinctly remember when I started to develop the attitude that I would rather be dead than live a mediocre life. It is now or never!

Stop procrastinating and get what you desire! Placing time limits on areas of your life will force you to establish that sense of urgency. You are creating this game plan in each chapter to give yourself a sense of responsibility and accountability. It is also to ensure that the necessary steps are completed each day to get you to your ultimate desire in building your Personal Brand.

Take action today and stay focused on the task at hand. Realize what is at the end of the tunnel. See the end result! How badly do you really want it? How urgent is it to you?

Visualize the end result. How urgent is it to me?

What will I put timelines on in my life starting today so that my Personal Brand makes the impact and income I desire?

LESSON THIRTY
WHAT YOU SHOW YOU SHALL REAP

"BE NOT DECEIVED; GOD IS NOT MOCKED: FOR WHATSOEVER A MAN SOWETH, THAT SHALL HE ALSO REAP."
GALATIANS 6:7

This is not just some spiritual saying from the Bible but a universal law in life. I have found it to be very true in many different aspects of life. "What you sow, you will reap." If you sow badly, you will reap badly; if you sow well, you will reap well. If all you eat is junk food, you will reap the negative effects of that junk food. If you sow the time to close more sales, you will close more sales. If you want to have a better relationship, invest the time to sow good seed into that relationship. As you start to follow the game plan, you will reap the benefits of being one step closer each day to your goal.

How much time are you sowing into getting what you want? How much effort are you sowing into your daily action step to get what you desire?

It's not just about doing it but doing it the right way. You've probably heard it said: practice makes perfect. Not necessarily! Practice makes permanent. Practicing the right way makes perfect. Perfect practice makes perfect! Are you sowing the right seed? Are you practicing the RIGHT way? Stop wasting your time staying busy and start investing your time wisely by being productive! Start today to make sure that you are sowing the

RIGHT seed on a daily basis to help you to reap the ultimate reward.

If You Want Something You've Never Had, You've Got To Do Something You've Never Done!

Take Action!

Am I sowing good seed on a daily basis to get what I desire?

What can I do better or more of to reap what I desire?

What am I going to do that I've never done so that I can get what I've never had?

LESSON THIRTY-ONE
GOALS

"SETTING GOALS IS THE FIRST STEP IN TURNING THE INVISIBLE INTO THE VISIBLE."
ANTHONY ROBBINS

If you don't know what you want, you will never get it. If you don't know where you are going, you will never get there. Setting goals will help lead you to where you want to go in life. Knowing where you want to go will enable you to concentrate your daily activities, actions, and efforts on the things that are necessary to get there.

Very few people set short-term goals. How much money do you want to make in the next 90 days, how many sales do you need to close in the next 30 days to build your tribe? These short-term goals are the small rewards leading to the big prize at the end. Once you have determined these short-term goals, the question is: what do you need to do on a daily basis? What about on a weekly basis? Or even a monthly and annual basis to get to this ultimate goal? Goal setting is crucial, but without the game plan to get you there, you will never complete those goals. In this book, starting today, you are going to set goals to build your Personal Brand, get your irresistible offer out to your dream clients, serve them so that they can move away from their pain and towards their pleasure, and turn this into a highly profitable business.

My Ultimate Goal for my Personal Brand is

and I will accomplish this by_____(date)

My 1-year Goal is

and I will accomplish this by_____(date)

My 30-day Goal is

LESSON THIRTY-TWO
SPEAK IT

"ALL OUR DREAMS CAN COME TRUE IF WE HAVE THE COURAGE TO PURSUE THEM"
WALT DISNEY

This is always a difficult step for people to do. I want you to begin to speak those things that you desire and want to accomplish in life. Let me start by saying that I don't believe you can just repeatedly say that you want something and it will happen. I am talking about speaking with a confidence and a positive attitude, while at the same time believing without a doubt that those things that you are taking action on will come to pass. If you repeatedly say, "I am going to lose those 20 pounds!" Then you will subconsciously find ways to make yourself lose those 20 pounds. You will start to believe that it is already a reality; therefore, you'll do what's necessary to make it happen. There is tremendous power in your words, my friend. This can work against you also if you allow it to. If you keep saying, "I'll never lose these 20 pounds," you won't make any effort, and you will eventually quit because your subconscious mind will have accepted that you will never lose the weight.

The other reason I believe that this is so powerful is that you will have people who will speak against you accomplishing your goal and building your Personal Brand, people who do not want you to succeed, and people who will doubt that you can do it. The way to counteract this negativity is for you to defeat them by speaking what you desire into existence. When you speak against this negativity, you are releasing your confidence, and you are exposing yourself to positive energy. You will never really experience true success in your life if you are negative and are always speaking depressing and doubtful things. When you constantly speak negatively, it will make you unpleasant to be around and very unhappy. Who wants to be around those kinds of people? I am a big action guy, and you should feel confident to do this because you are putting action behind the words! Here is the cool thing: speaking your goal into existence can considerably improve your results and how you feel about yourself and others.

It goes back to the premise that what you sow is what you will reap. Now, why is this so powerful for you? It is because you are not only speaking it, but you are putting action behind it while you speak it. Here's what I mean: I want you to not just speak it, but SPEAK IT WITH AUTHORITY. Say it like you mean it. Use the tones and pitches in your voice; use the non-verbal communication of your body language to express what you really want. Speak it with visualization and imagination and start to see that very thing that you are speaking! That is what the game plan is all about, and that is a powerful combination!

It always makes me laugh when someone says that there is no power in words. Think about it for a second... Think about something someone said to you as a kid that was hurtful. Chances are you can probably recall something that was said. You have never forgotten it! In fact, it may even still bother you. Maybe someone told you that you couldn't do something, and then you started to think that maybe you couldn't, and it stopped you from accomplishing something in your life. On the flip side, has anyone ever said something so positive to you that it encouraged you to take a step in your life that you were afraid to take? I know that this has happened to me.

There's Power in Your Words!

Create your 'I am' Statement today and start to say it each day with Authority, with Visualization, with Imagination! Your 'I am' Statement is who you are, your Personal Brand, the impact you will make, the people you will serve, and the money you will make.

LESSON THIRTY-THREE
MAKE THE DECISION

> **"ARE YOU WILLING TO SACRIFICE WHAT YOU WANT MOST IN LIFE FOR WHAT IS COOL, EASY, COMFORTABLE, SEXY AND CONVENIENT AT THE MOMENT?"**
> **COACH JC**

How badly do you really want it? How badly do you really want to build your PURPOSE-DRIVEN, HIGHLY PROFITABLE PERSONAL BRAND? How badly do you really want to have success in life? How badly do you really want to make your greatest impact? How badly do you really want to create financial freedom? Well, I have great news for you. Now you can; Now is your time! You may be saying to yourself, "It is just not that simple coach." Of course it is. All it takes is one choice. Just one decision – made by you!

A big part of you WINNING in life is about routine, being consistent in just getting the things that need to be done, done! Many people get complacent and comfortable and get stuck. If you are not careful, it is very easy to fall into this trap of mediocrity and just go through life rather than LIVE LIFE. Make a decision starting today that you are not going to live another day on cruise control. Make a decision today that you are not going to allow your life to become stagnant.

Have some passion about who you are, and make the decision to be passionate about what you are doing. It's your choice! Yes, it is that simple. So many people allow others to make decisions for them on a daily basis; they allow people to choose their future for them. Not me and not you! You may not have the perfect body, you may not have the perfect job, you may not live in the perfect environment, but remember, you can still choose to change any of that. It is just a choice, just one decision!

Today, you are choosing to take control of your life by creating your new reality. By doing life on your terms! To no longer hate what you do and just go through Today, you are choosing to take control of your life by taking control of your financial freedom, your time freedom. By building your Personal Brand! You choose! You choose your THOUGHTS! You choose your ATTITUDE. You choose your ACTIONS. You choose your RESULTS. You choose what your life looks like. You get to choose just about everything that happens on a daily basis. You choose who you are. It's YOUR choice!

Starting today, I want you to make a decision. Make the decision that your life is valuable and that you are worth it. You are done thinking about it! Starting today, you will no longer make excuses, and you will no longer accept anything else but greatness. You will no longer accept anything but results! Start to make some big choices that are going to lead to big results. You must make a decision, a choice, to create an opportunity in your life that you may not have had otherwise. You will do that by choosing to build your Personal Brand!

What choice will I make today that will take me closer to my goal?

What choice will I make today that I will do every day to get me closer to my goal?

LESSON THIRTY-FOUR
MAKE THE DECISION

"DO IT, AND THEN YOU WILL FEEL MOTIVATED TO DO IT"
ZIG ZIGLAR

Now it is your time! You have learned in this book how to build your Personal Brand, how to take your skillset, your wisdom, your knowledge and teach it to your dream clients so that you can make your greatest impact and profit. But most importantly you have also learned how to create the WINNING mindset, to transform your thinking, take massive action each day, and have anything you want any time you want it.

I have discovered that most of the time the one thing holding people back is their own limiting beliefs. That is why throughout this book, as you are building your personal brand, we take time to breakthrough many of those limiting beliefs. YOU are your personal brand! You have to BE YOUR BEST to give YOUR BEST!

You have the WINNING mindset, you have built your Personal Brand. There is just one more thing left... JUST DO IT! Like our friends at Nike say, JUST DO IT!

It's simple. It really is... if you just do it! All you need to do is stay focused on the end result, your "WHY" and do the simple, disciplined things each day.

I want for you now to commit to not just doing it, but to doing it in the best way that you possibly can. To play ALL OUT! No more average! No more mediocre! So many people do things half-heartedly and just cruise through life. Build your Personal Brand like your life depends on it! Go ALL IN!

I want you to really think about this: in just a short time, as you went through this game plan you built your Personal Brand! Now it's time to get your message to the world, reach your dream clients that you were called to serve, help them stop the pain in their life and bring them to their heaven, and at the same time build your life the way you want! Can you give it everything that you've got? Can you not just do it, but do it like there is no tomorrow? Is your life worth it? Actions speak louder than words: Show me what you've got! Just Do It!!!

Today I want you to go back to page one and start to refine all your daily action steps from each chapter. Go back and make sure you were ALL IN. That you played ALL OUT! Go back and refine what needs to be refined, redo what needs to be redone, take the time to create your Personal Brand!

CONGRATULATIONS!

You did it! You built your Personal Brand so that you can do what you love, make your greatest impact and make money doing it. You are creating your new reality in business and in life.

The steps that you have just gone through are simple, and they work if you just work them. WINNING is not some big event that just happens. It comes down to you executing your daily action steps and exercising the law of WINNING in your life. No one else can do it for you. Time can work for you or against you! What's your choice? How badly do you want to WIN?

I believe in you and know that you desperately want it. Listen to me, don't get overwhelmed, just follow the game plan and execute the simple, disciplined things every day that will get you to the promise land!

So, where do you go from here?

5 Steps To Set Yourself Up To WIN:

1. Create your Ascension Model. With your irresistible offer it is time to create your service or product ascension model around your wisdom, knowledge and skillset. What will be your front end offer, your backend offer, your upsells and downsells?

2. Build Your Business Blueprint. Now it is time to turn your Personal Brand into a business and start to make money.

3. Live It Out. Start to live out your brand. Let everyone know what you do and how you do it and live your purpose and passion out on a daily basis.

4. Market. Time to get your message to the world baby! Create your lead generation strategy on how you will acquire customers/clients and where the best places are to find your dream clients. (social media is a great place to start)

5. Apply To Work With Us. You can take the fast track, take your Personal Brand and turn it into a business, start marketing right away so that you can make your greatest impact and income. How? Through our WIN ALL DAY Personal Branding Mastermind or WIN ALL DAY Personal Branding 1-on-1 Coaching. Apply Now at www.coachjc.com

PURPOSE. PASSION. PROFIT.

Coach JC

Jonathan Conneely, Coach JC, is available for speaking engagements at any conference or school. For more information, please contact:

Coach JC
JJC Enterprises
8177 S Harvard Ave.
Suite 420
Tulsa, OK 74137

918-760-2206
Email: jc@coachjc.com
website: www.CoachJC.com

I Would Love to Hear from YOU!

I know this book has changed your life! I would love to hear from you. Please write to me as I would love to hear how it has touched your life.

ABOUT JONATHAN CONNEELY

COACH JC

COACH JC IS AN ENTREPRENEUR, AUTHOR, MOTIVATIONAL SPEAKER, AND BUSINESS AND LIFE COACH.

He is the author of 4 books and has motivated audiences of all sizes through his professional speaking, including opening up for President Donald J Trump during his presidential campaign and being coined, "Trumps Hype Man".

Coach JC has empowered thousands of people to WIN in life through his books, speaking, podcasts, coaching and social media presence. He has coached and consulted professional athletes from the NFL, NBA, MLB, MLS, WNBA, and Olympians,CEO's and Pastors.

As an entrepreneur Coach JC has launched 4 companies within the personal development and business arena. He has been recognized as a 30 under 30,40 under 40,The Best of The Best, and The Young Entrepreneur of the year. Coach JC started the Non-Profit, Fit First Responders now serving over 85 first responding agencies.

Coach JC went from down and out, over $400k in debt to discover how to experience true health, wealth and happiness and now shares that message world-wide. After building his Personal Brand, using Social Media to grow his brands Coach JC became a go-to for helping other's build their Purpose Driven, Highly Profitable Personal Brand.

He is the creator and founder of the WIN ALL DAY Movement, WIN ALL DAY Academy, WIN ALL DAY Strength, WIN ALL DAY Personal Branding Academy and coaches and consults others to WIN IN LIFE.

Coach JC's greatest accomplishments are the ladies in his life, his wife Jodi, his daughter Alivia, his mom and his sister.

APPLY TO GET ACCESS TO BECOME PART OF THE WIN ALL DAY ACADEMY AND BUILD YOUR PURPOSE DRIVEN, HIGHLY PROFITABLE PERSONAL BRAND.

WWW.WINALLDAYPERSONALBRAND.COM

REQUEST COACH JC FOR YOUR EVENT

Jonathan Conneely, Coach JC, is available for speaking engagements at conferences, departments and agencies.

ORGANIZATIONS BRING IN COACH JC TO SPEAK ON THE TOPICS OF:

Leadership | Teamwork
Motivation | Culture Development
Mental Conditioning | Personal Branding

TO MAKE COACH JC A PART OF YOUR NEXT EVENT PLEASE CONTACT US:

1-800-382-1506
email: info@coachjc.com

www.CoachJC.com

WIN ALL DAY BOOK SERIES

Learn how to :

- Create your purpose driven, highly profitable brand.

- Create the winning mindset to achieve ulitmate success in life.

- Look, feel and perform your best with a 27 day gameplan.

- Create the winning mindset to win as an athlete and win in life.

GET YOURS TODAY AT WWW.COACHJC.COM

Our Father who art in heaven,
hallowed be thy name.
Thy kingdom come.
Thy will be done on earth
as it is in heaven.
Give us this day our daily bread,
and forgive us our trespasses,
as we forgive those who trespass against us,
and lead us not into temptation,
but deliver us from evil.
For thine is the kingdom,
and the power, and the glory,
for ever and ever.
Amen.

www.ingramcontent.com/pod-product-compliance
Lightning Source LLC
Chambersburg PA
CBHW051452290426
44109CB00016B/1732